MAP SKILLS

REM 128

A TEACHING RESOURCE FROM

©2007
**Copyright by Remedia Publications, Inc.
All Rights Reserved. Printed in the U.S.A.**

To find Remedia products in a store near you, visit:
www.rempub.com/stores

REMEDIA PUBLICATIONS, INC.
15887 N. 76ᵗᴴ STREET • SUITE 120 • SCOTTSDALE, AZ • 85260

**RESEARCH-BASED ACTIVITIES
Supports State & National Standards**

This product utilizes innovative strategies and proven methods to improve student learning. The product is based upon reliable research and effective practices that have been replicated in classrooms across the United States. Information regarding the research basis is provided on our website at www.rempub.com/research

Introduction

MAP SKILLS is designed to give students ample practice with the basic skills of using maps. Each topic begins with a relatively easy activity and progresses to more difficult practice on the same topic.

Both fictional and actual maps have been used throughout. This allows students to understand that mapping is more than road maps and globes.

Upon completion of the activities in this book, students should be able to:

- •use accurate directional words and indicators.

- •verbalize locations in relationship to other locations.

- •recognize picture symbols used on maps.

- •identify routes from place to place.

- •use a grid effectively in locating position.

- •construct a simple map with a legend.

- •interpret the information given on different types of maps.

The activities in this book may be reproduced for use with students in the classroom.

It is not easy to get somewhere unless you know:

1. the direction you are facing.
2. the direction you want to go.

A compass will help you. A compass shows direction.

Most maps have a compass printed on them to show direction.

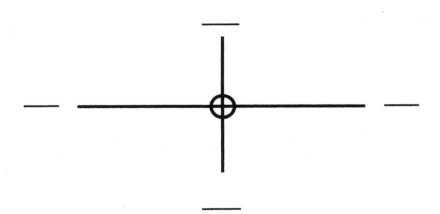

Letters are used to tell the directions on a compass.

N = North   E = East   S = South   W = West

Do the following activities:

1. North is *always* the top of a map. Put an "N" on the compass to show "North."

2. If you stand facing North, East will be on your right. Put an "E" on the compass to show "East."

3. South is opposite North. South is at the _____ of the map. Put an "S" on the compass.

4. Put a "W" to show "West." If you face North, West will be on your _____ .

Use the compass to answer these questions.

1. If you are facing South, East will be to your _____.

2. If you face _____, West will be to your right.

3. If you face East, West will be _____ you.

4. If you face _____, North will be to your right.

Write the letters to show the directions on this compass.

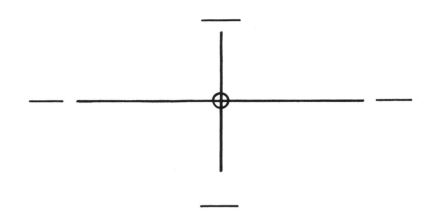

Sometimes we need more directions than N, S, E, W. We can add four more directions to the compass.

We place the directions <u>between</u> those we already have.

For example: Between North and West, we would put Northwest (NW). Between South and East, we would put Southeast (SE)

Write in the letters to show all the directions on this compass rose.

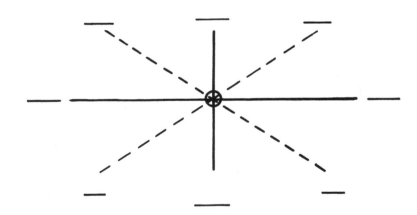

Write the full name for the letters used on the compass rose.

1. N = _____

2. E = _____

3. NE = _____

4. S = _____

5. W = _____

6. SW = _____

7. SE = _____

8. NW = _____

Imagine a compass with the pond in the center. Write in the letters to show all the directions on this compass.

1. The tiger is _____ of the giraffe.

2. The bear would go _____ to reach the zebra.

3. If the lion walked **east**, he would meet the _____ .

4. To reach the pond, the zebra must go _____ .

5. If the elephant walked **south**, he would meet the _____ .

6. The giraffe is _____ of the pond.

7. To get to the lion, the tiger would walk _____ to the pond

   and turn _____ .

8. The monkey went _____ to the pond. Then, he turned south.

   He ran into the _____ .

9. Explain how the giraffe could get to the bear.

   _____

3

Compass directions are very important on maps. If a map shows a small space or a huge space, we use compass directions.

Harvey Hamster's Home

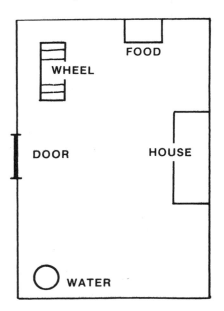

Use direction words to finish these sentences.

1. If Harvey goes from the food to the water, he will travel _____ .

2. To get from the door to his house, Harvey will travel _____ .

3. If Harvey goes from his house to the exercise wheel, he will go _____ .

4. To get from the exercise wheel to the water bottle, he must go _____ .

5. If he goes from the door to the food dish, he is going _____ .

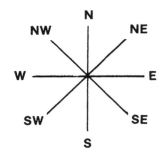

This map shows a much larger space than a hamster cage. Use the direction words to finish these sentences.

1. To go from Logan to Richfield, you will travel _____ .

2. If you are going to Dry Fork from Trout Creek, you will go _____ .

3. Richfield is southeast of _____
    _____ .

4. The **eastern** side of Utah borders on the state of _____ .

5. The direction from Moab to Cedar City is _____ .

6. The Colorado River cuts across the _____ corner of Utah.

7. If you go **north** from Richfield, you will come to what city? _____

4

When two streets cross, they form an **intersection**.

Each intersection has four corners. We name the corners by the directions.

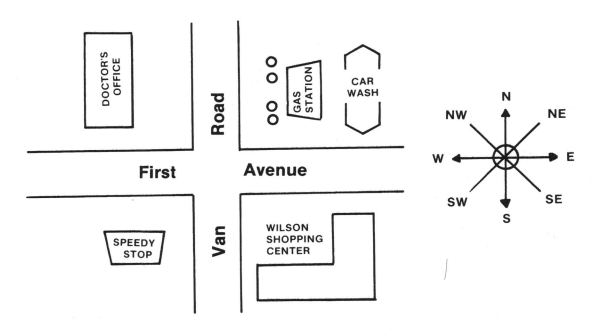

On the map above, you see the intersection of First Avenue and Van Road. The gas station is on the **northeast** corner.

1. In what directions does Van Road run? _____

2. On which corner is Wilson Shopping Center? _____

3. What is on the **southwest** corner?

   _____

4. In what directions does First Avenue run? _____

5. If you were going **south** on Van Road, which direction would you turn to get gas?

   _____

6. On which corner is the doctor's office? _____

7. What direction would you go to get from Speedy Stop to the shopping center?

   _____

8. If you are going **south** on Van Road, which direction would you turn to go to the doctor's office?

   _____

Maps are small drawings of places. Symbols are used to show the important things on a map. Symbols are simple pictures that mean certain things.

Match these symbols with the words from the box that tell what they mean.

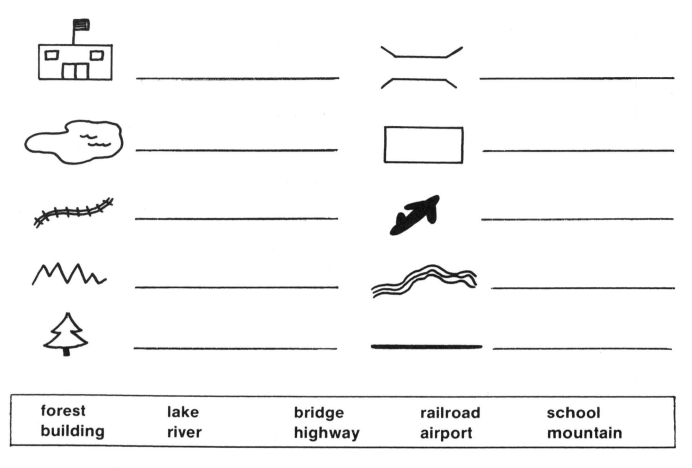

forest	lake	bridge	railroad	school
building	river	highway	airport	mountain

Here are some other symbols you should know.

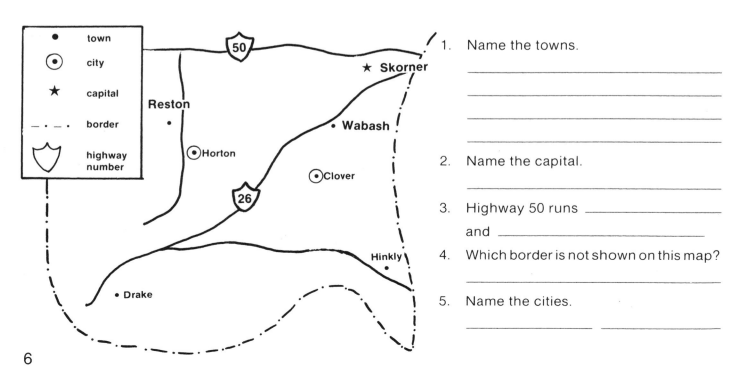

1. Name the towns.

   _____

   _____

   _____

   _____

2. Name the capital.

   _____

3. Highway 50 runs _____

   and _____

4. Which border is not shown on this map?

   _____

5. Name the cities.

   _____

The box which describes the symbols on a map is called a **legend**.

Use the legend and the map to answer the questions below.

CITY MAP OF BOUNTY

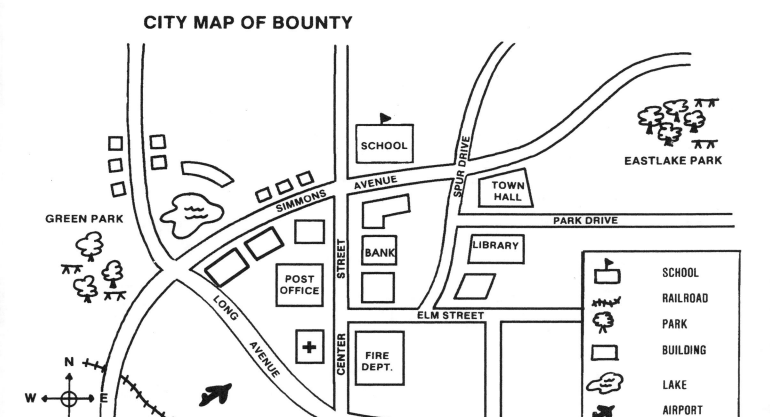

1. The school is on the corner of _____

   and _____ .

2. Green Park is _____ of the Post Office.

3. The directions the railroad travels are _____ and _____ .

4. Mrs. Brown's class is going to the lake for a picnic.

   They will go _____ .

5. Most of the buildings are _____ of Simmons Avenue.

6. There are _____ parks in Bounty.

7. To get from the library to the Town Hall, you will go _____ .

8. If you are going south on Center Street, you will turn and travel _____
   to go to the airport.

Use the legend and follow the directions below to finish the map.

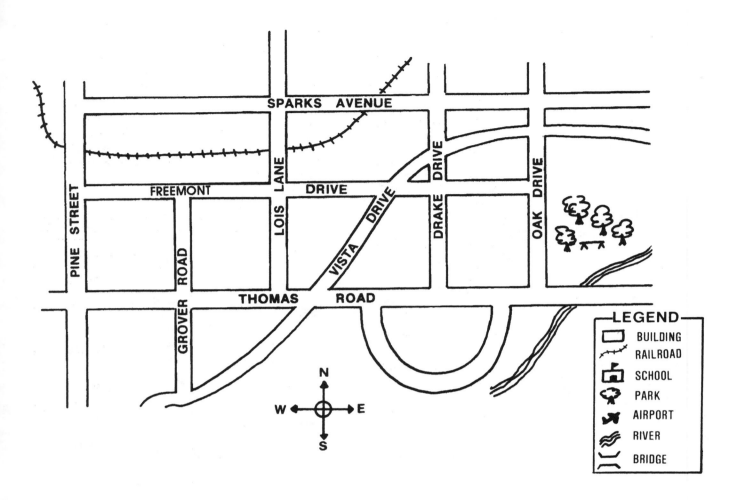

1. Put a discount store on the **southeast** corner of Grover Road and Thomas Road.

2. Write the name on the street you think should be named **New Circle Drive**.

3. Make the railroad station on Sparks Avenue, just **north** of the railroad and **east** of Lois Lane.

4. The school is on the **southwest** corner of Lois Lane and Freemont Drive. Draw it on the map.

5. Put the airport **north** of Sparks Avenue and **east** of Oak Drive.

6. Make a **bridge** where the river crosses under Thomas Road.

7. Make another park on the **northeast** corner of Pine Street and Thomas Road.

8. Make an **apartment house** on Oak Drive, just north of Freemont.

Draw a town! This is a street map of a small town. As you can see, there is nothing here but streets! This town needs homes, stores, parks, schools, and much more!

Draw at least six different things on the map. Make a legend in the box to explain your symbols.

This is a map of _____ .

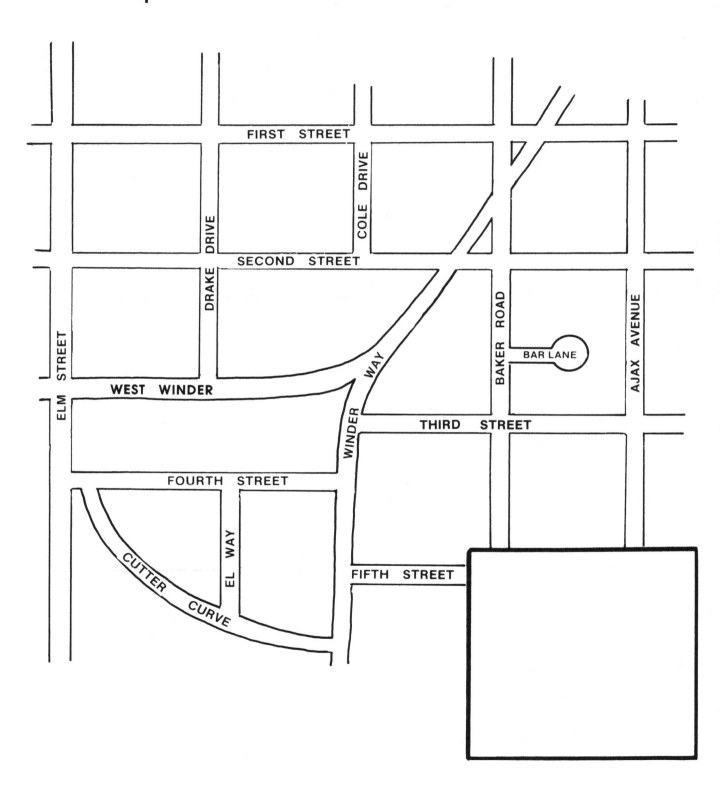

Use the legend and the map to answer the questions below.

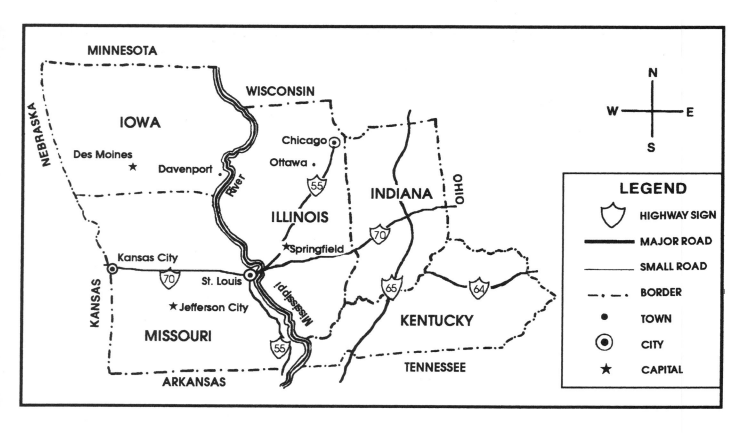

1. The border between Iowa and Missouri runs in what directions? _____

2. Highway 70 (E & W) goes through which 3 states?

_____

3. What is the capital city of Iowa? _____

4. Is Ottawa, Illinois, a large city or a town? _____

5. Which highway would you take to get from Chicago, Illinois, to St. Louis,

Missouri? _____

6. Two highways go through Kentucky. What are they?

_____

7. What highway would take you from Kansas City to St. Louis, Missouri? _____

8. The southern border of Missouri is next to what state? _____

9. What river forms the border between Missouri and Illinois? _____

10. What is the capital city of Missouri? _____

Use the map and the legend to answer the questions about the city of New Rapids.

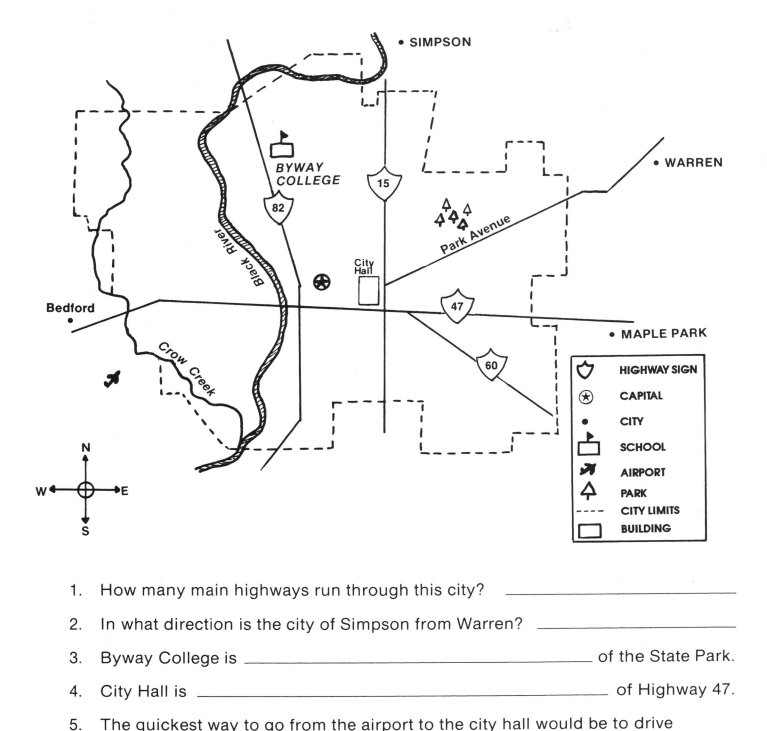

1. How many main highways run through this city? _____

2. In what direction is the city of Simpson from Warren? _____

3. Byway College is _____ of the State Park.

4. City Hall is _____ of Highway 47.

5. The quickest way to go from the airport to the city hall would be to drive

    _____ on Highway 47, then turn left on _____ .

6. What is the name of the river that flows north to south? _____

7. What cities are east of New Rapids? _____

    and _____

11

Use the map to answer the questions below.

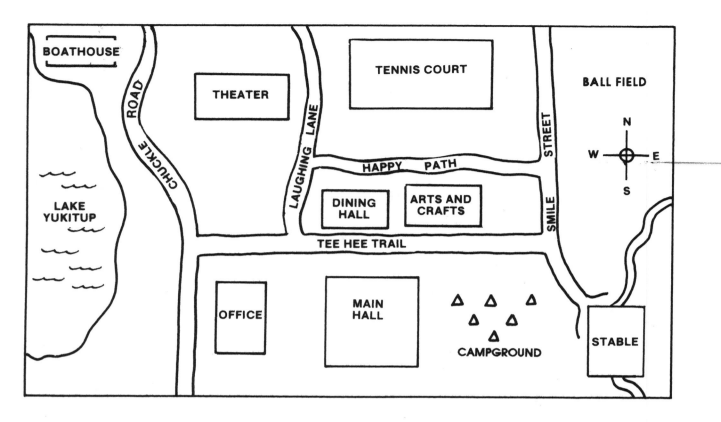

1. What is just **west** of the campground? _____

2. On which side of the theater is Laughing Lane? _____

3. If you walked along Tee Hee Trail from Chuckle Road to the stables, in which direction would you be going?

   _____

4. Keeping on a trail or path, in which directions can you walk from Laughing Lane?

   _____

5. What would be the fastest way to get from the boathouse to the main hall?

   _____

6. Which building is just **east** of the dining hall? _____

7. Which building is **farthest** from the theater? _____

8. If you were walking along Happy Path and the arts and crafts building was on your left, which way would you be going?

   _____

9. The area just **east** of Smile Street is a _____ .

Use the map to answer these questions.

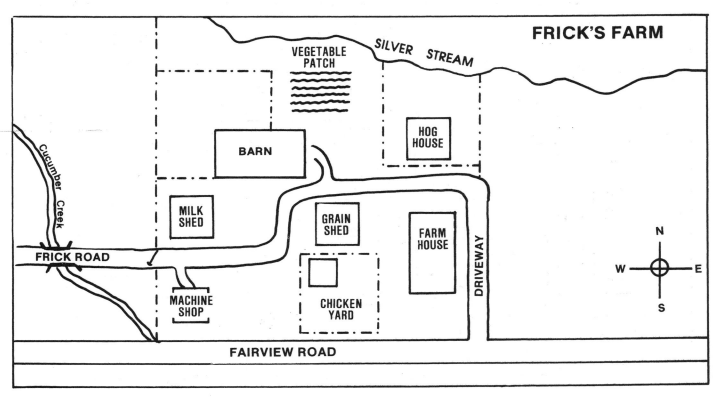

1. What is the name of the road that runs on the south side of the farm?

   _____

2. The farmhouse faces the driveway. What direction is that? _____

3. The building nearest to Silver Stream is _____ .

4. If you walked from the milk shed to the farmhouse, the barn would be on your

   _____ .

5. Where Frick Road crosses Cucumber Creek, there is a _____ .

6. The chicken house is _____ of the grain shed.

7. The symbol __ . __ . __ on the map probably means a _____ .

8. To get from the vegetable patch to the hog house, you would walk

   _____ .

9. The milk shed is _____ of the barn.

10. The machine shop is _____ of the chicken yard.

Use the map to answer the questions below.

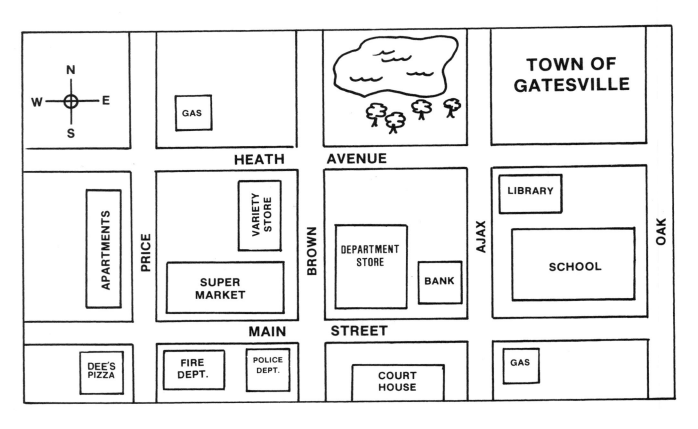

1. On the map of _____ , the street farthest **south**

   is _____ .

2. If you walked **down** Main Street from Oak to Ajax, you would be walking

   _____ .

3. The building **nearest** the fire department is the _____ .

4. The bank is on the **northwest** corner of _____

   and _____ .

5. Which is **larger** — the bank or the library?

   _____

6. What building is **west** of the school? _____

7. Dee's Pizza is on the _____ side of Main Street.

8. The **library** is on the _____ corner of _____

   and _____ .

9. The **school** is _____ of the courthouse.

10. On the **southwest** corner of Heath and Brown is a _____ .

14

Use the map of Dillyburg and the legend to answer the questions below.

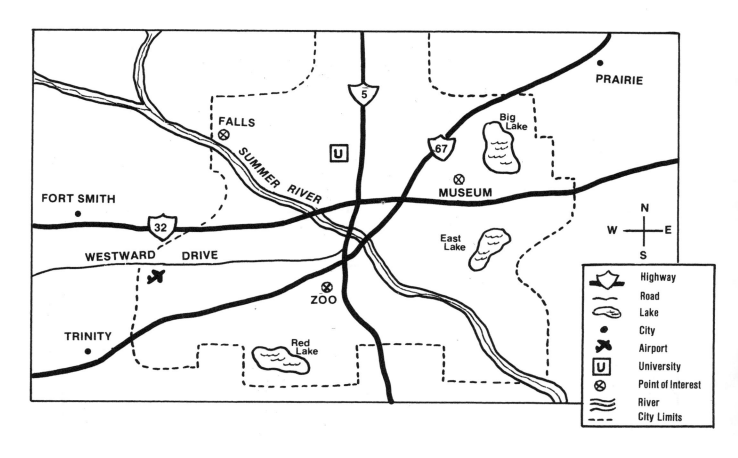

1. What lake is in the **northeastern** part of Dillyburg? _____

2. The symbol – – – – – – – shows the _____ of Dillyburg.

3. To get to the airport from the university, you would probably take Highway

    _____ and turn _____ on Westward Drive.

4. If you were traveling **through** Dillyburg from the **northeast**, you would probably stay

    on Highway _____ .

5. The best way to go **through** Dillyburg from west to east would be on

    Highway _____ .

6. How many lakes are there in Dillyburg? _____

7. The university is _____ of Highway 5.

8. There are three points of interest in Dillyburg. They are the:

    _____   _____

    _____

This is a map of a nice little vacation spot. It is named Sunny Beach. Use the map to answer the questions.

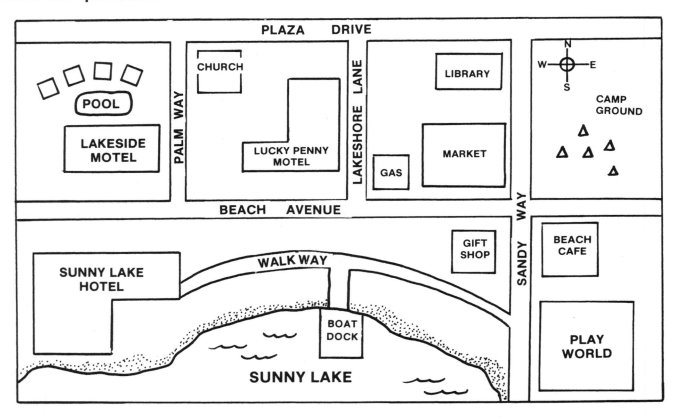

1. Playworld is on the **east** side of _____ .

2. On which side of Lakeshore Lane is the Lucky Penny Motel? _____

3. What is the main street in Sunny Beach? _____

4. Where would you rent a room to be **closest** to the beach?

   _____

5. How many places are there to rent rooms? _____

6. What building is **nearest** the library? _____

7. If you were standing on the boat dock and facing the Beach Cafe, what direction would

   you be looking? _____

8. What is on the **northeast** corner of Beach Avenue and Lakeshore Lane?

   _____

9. What street is on the **north** side of the campgrounds? _____

10. On what corner is the gift shop? _____

A zoo is a wonderful place to explore! Most zoos have many paths to take you to the different animal areas. You could spend a lot of time looking for the monkeys and never find them! A map is the answer.

Use the map to answer the questions below.

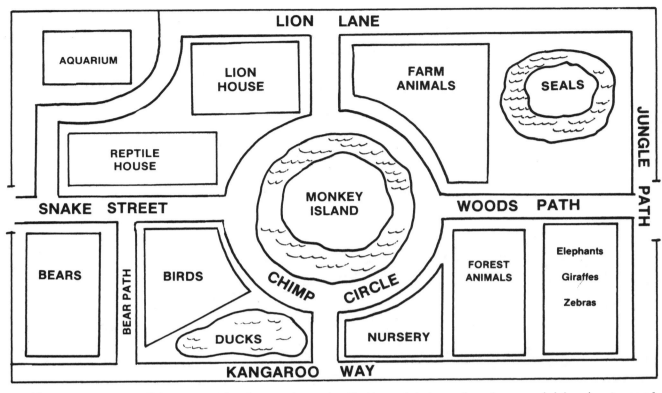

1. If you were walking **south** along Jungle Path, which animals would be just **west** of you? _____

2. Which animals have ponds for swimming? _____

3. If you walked **east** on Lion Lane, which way would you turn to get to the giraffes?

   _____

4. What is the name of the path around Monkey Island?

   _____

5. What would you find on the **north** side of Snake Street?

   _____

6. Which animals would you find in the **northwest** corner of the zoo?

   _____

7. The baby animals are _____ of the forest animals.

8. Where would you go to see a python? _____

Use the map and the legend to answer the questions below.

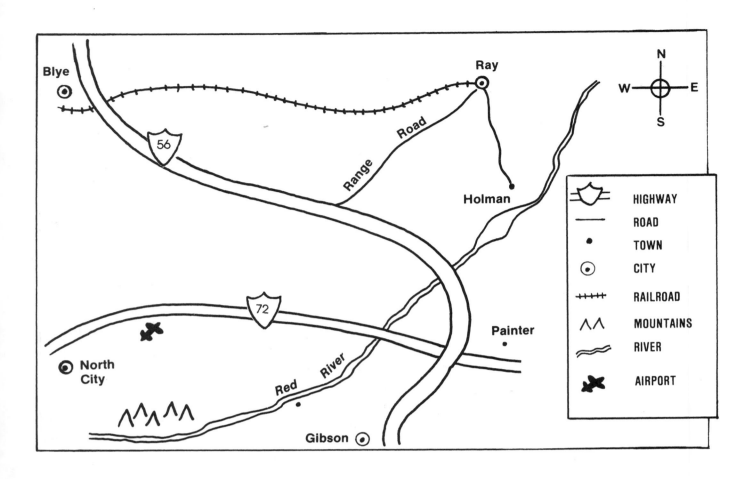

1. To get from Blye to Gibson, you would use _____ .

2. The two highways cross _____ of the river.

3. You could go by train from _____ to _____ .

4. The airport is on Highway _____ .

5. What are the names of the cities?

   _____   _____

   _____   _____

6. Painter is _____ of Holman.

7. Highway 72 runs by what city? _____

8. To reach Ray from Blye, you would turn _____ off of Highway 56

   onto _____ .

This is an unfinished map of Dogood's Dude Ranch. Read the directions below to finish the map.

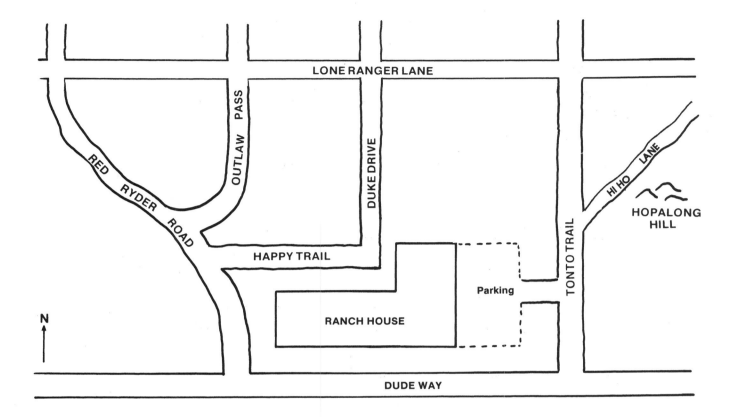

1. The Dude Ranch takes its guests on cook-outs. They have a big barbecue pit just **southwest** of Hopalong Hill. Draw the pit on the map.

2. The stables are on the **northwest** corner of Red Ryder Road and Dude Way.

3. The corral is a fenced area just **west** of the stables.

4. The Chuck House is **north** of the ranch house near Duke Drive.

5. A riding and rodeo arena is **between** Red Ryder Road and Outlaw Pass.

6. Sometimes, guests go on overnight camp-outs. The campgrounds are **northeast** of Tonto Trail and Lone Ranger Lane. Show the campgrounds.

7. The tennis courts are **between** Outlaw Pass and Duke Drive. They are **north** of Happy Trail.

8. Six-Shooter Lake is directly **east** of the ranch house — **east** of Tonto Trail.

9. There is a hiking path from Hopalong Hill to the lake.

10. Just **north** of the Chuck House are the 3 cabins where the ranch hands live.

This map of Washington, D.C., shows many of the interesting places to visit. The legend tells you what each building is. The dotted lines show the route of the Metrorail through the city.

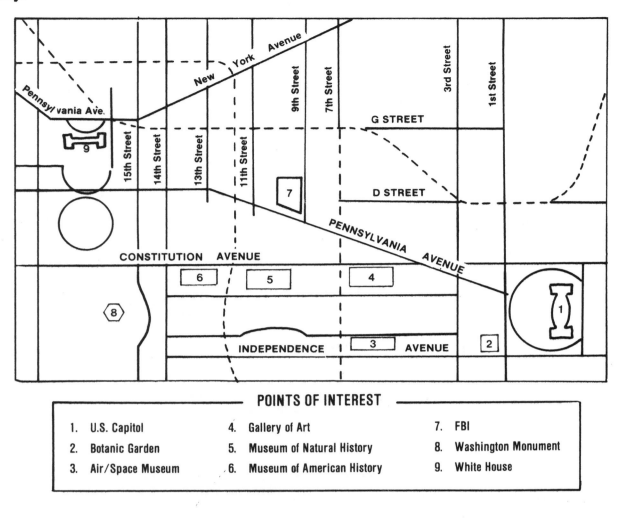

POINTS OF INTEREST

1. U.S. Capitol
2. Botanic Garden
3. Air/Space Museum
4. Gallery of Art
5. Museum of Natural History
6. Museum of American History
7. FBI
8. Washington Monument
9. White House

1. The Botanic Garden is on the corner of _____
   and _____ .

2. The **lettered** streets run in what directions? _____

3. On what corner is the FBI building?
   _____

4. If you were riding the Metrorail, at what street would you get off to go to the Museum of
   Natural History? _____

5. The **numbered** streets run _____ and _____ .

6. The Botanic Garden is near what large building? _____

7. The Museum of Natural History is between what two buildings?
   _____ and _____

8. The street in front of the White House is _____ .

The Fritter Family went to Bunkerfun, an amusement park in their home town of Bunkerville. Answer the questions below. Then, draw a line showing the route the Fritter Family took through Bunkerfun.

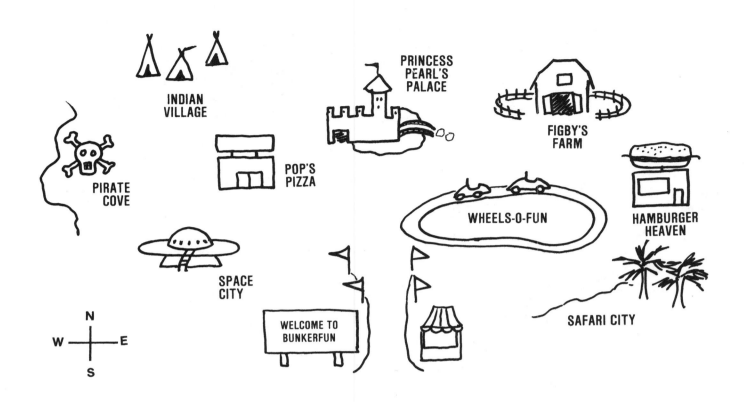

1. As they entered the park, they turned **west** and went to _____ .

2. When they came out, they walked **northwest** to _____ .

3. Fred got a little teepee at their next stop, which was _____ .

4. Flossie was hungry so they walked **south** to _____ .

5. Their next stop was the Palace. They entered on the _____ side

   and left by the bridge on the _____ side.

6. Fred wanted some excitement! They walked **southeast** to _____ .

7. To keep Flossie happy, they walked _____ to pet the farm animals at

   _____ .

8. They were all hungry, so they headed _____ to Hamburger Heaven.

9. Their last stop was Safari City. They got there by walking _____ .

10. From Safari City, they walked _____ to the main gate.

Below is a map of the United States. Use the map to answer the questions below.

1. The Great Lakes are on the border between _____
    and the United States.

    The names of the Great Lakes are:

    _____   _____

    _____   _____

    _____

2. What ocean is **west** of the United States? _____

3. What state is **north** of Wyoming? _____

4. Which states border the Gulf of Mexico?

    _____   _____

    _____   _____

    _____

5. Which two states are not connected to all the other states?

    _____   _____

This map shows the two halves of a globe. It shows the large land areas called "continents." There are seven continents.

The line on the globe is the "equator." It is an imaginary line that divides the earth into two "hemispheres." The Northern Hemisphere is the top half. The Southern Hemisphere is the bottom half. Use the map to answer the questions.

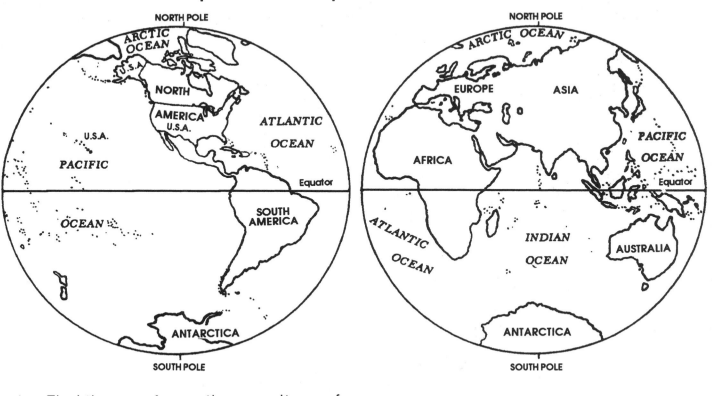

1. Find the **equator** on the map. It runs from _____

   to _____ .

2. At the very top of the globe is the _____ .

3. At the bottom is the _____

4. Write the names of the **seven continents** you see on the map.

   _____   _____

   _____   _____

   _____   _____

   _____

5. Write the names of the **four oceans** you see.

   _____   _____

   _____   _____

6. North America is in the _____ hemisphere.

Alaska

ARCTIC OCEAN

GREENLAND

UNITED STATES

PACIFIC OCEAN

Hudson Bay

CANADA

Gulf of St. Lawrence

Great Lakes

UNITED STATES

ATLANTIC OCEAN

MEXICO

Gulf of Mexico

CENTRAL AMERICA

SOUTH AMERICA

This is a map of the continent of North America. North America is the third largest continent on Earth. Use the map to answer the questions.

1. What two countries share the Great Lakes?

   _____   _____

2. List the countries found within the continent of North America.

   _____   _____

   _____   _____

3. What ocean borders the **east** side of North America? _____

4. What ocean borders the **west** side? _____

5. Mexico is _____ of the United States.

6. What country is between the United States and the state of Alaska?

   _____

7. What ocean is **north** of North America? _____

8. If you were traveling from Canada to the United States, in what direction would you be

   going? _____

24

Use the map to answer the questions below.

1.   What two continents are shown on this map?

     _____   _____

2.   South America is in the _____ hemisphere and

     the _____ hemisphere. Most of it is in the

     _____ hemisphere.

3.   South America is _____ of the continent of Antarctica.

4.   The ocean on the **eastern** coast is the _____ .

5.   The ocean on the **western** coast is the _____ .

6.   The country of Venezuela is in the _____ hemisphere.

7.   The largest country in South America is _____ .

8.   The country of Chile runs along the _____ coast of South America.

Use the map to answer the questions.

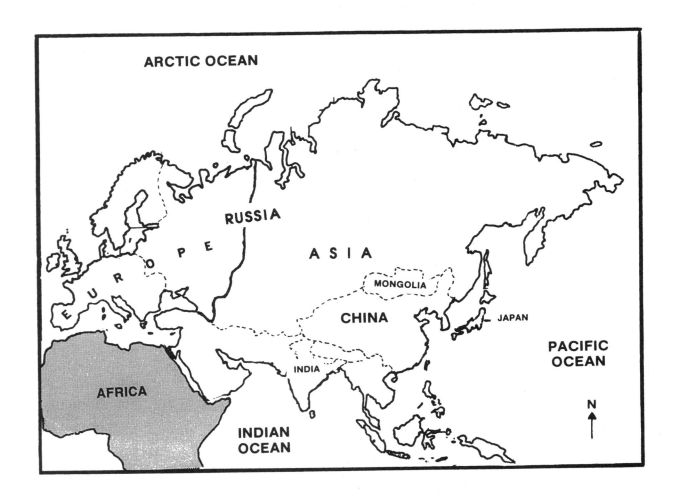

1. The two whole continents shown on this map are _____
   and _____ .

2. What country is on both continents? _____

3. Europe is _____ of Asia.

4. What three oceans border Asia? _____

   _____   _____

5. North of Europe is the _____ Ocean.

6. The largest country on this map is _____ .

7. Between China and Russia is the country of _____ .

8. What island is off the **east** coast of Asia? _____

9. What continent is **south** of Europe? _____

10. What country forms the **southern** tip of Asia? _____

Use the map to answer the questions.

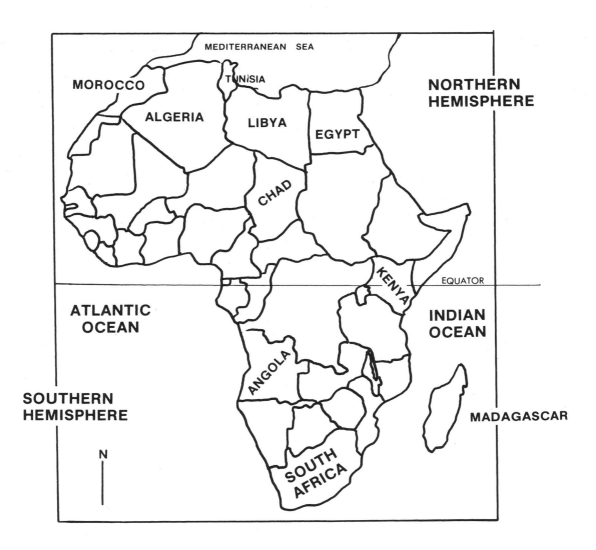

1. The continent shown on this map is _____ .

2. Most of this continent is in the _____ hemisphere.

3. The ocean on the **east** side of Africa is the _____ Ocean.

4. The _____ Sea forms the **northern** border.

5. The country on the southern tip is _____

6. The ocean on the **west** side of Africa is the _____ .

7. The island just **east** of Africa is _____ .

8. These countries are on the Mediterranean Sea:

   _____   _____

   _____   _____

   _____

Here is a world map. It would look like this if you peeled the outside off a globe and laid it out flat. Use the map to answer the questions.

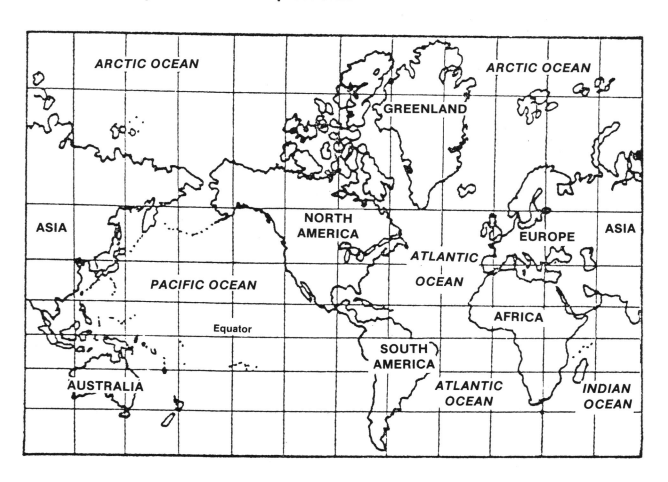

1. To travel from South America to Africa, in what direction would you travel?

   _____

2. What ocean would you cross? _____

3. To go from North America to Australia, in what direction would you travel?

   _____

4. What ocean would you cross? _____

5. Which ocean is north of Asia? _____

6. What ocean lies between Europe and North America? _____

7. On this map, what continent is the farthest **south**? _____

8. What continent is **north** of the Indian Ocean? _____

9. Through which two continents does the equator pass?

   _____

Sometimes, it is very hard to find places on a map. A GRID makes it easier.

Grid lines are drawn on a map. They are drawn from **west to east** and from **north to south**. The lines make **blocks of space** on a map.

Numbers are used to name the blocks **across the top**.

Letters are used to name the blocks **down the side**.

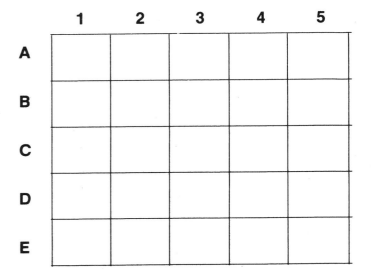

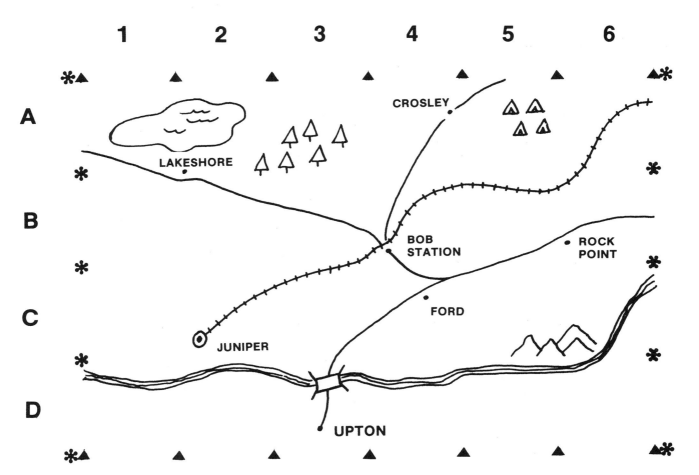

Use a ruler to draw grid lines on the map above.

Connect each ▲ at the top of the map to the ▲ at the bottom.

Now, connect each ✳ on the west side to the ✳ across from it on the east.

Does your grid on page 29 look like this? If it does, you followed directions well. Use the grid to locate places.

Each block is named by a letter and number.

Let's find **D4**. Put your finger on **D** at the side of the map. Move it across until you come to the block in the **4** column. This block is **D4**.

What do you find in D4 on the map? _____

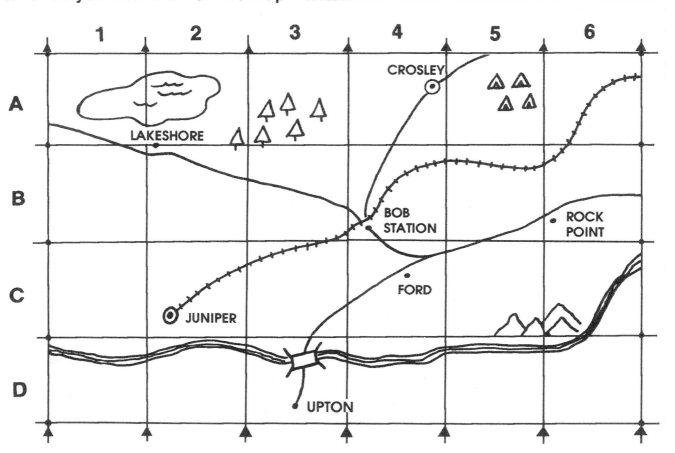

1. Find these blocks on the map. On the line, write what you see there.

   A2 _____   B3 _____

   C5 _____   A3 _____

2. List the blocks the railroad runs through.

   _____ _____ _____ _____ _____ _____ _____

3. In what block is the bridge? _____

4. Where do you find the campground? _____

5. Are there any towns in **C3**? _____

6. Where is Rock Point? _____

30

Here is a map of Loontown.

It has a grid over it to help you locate places.

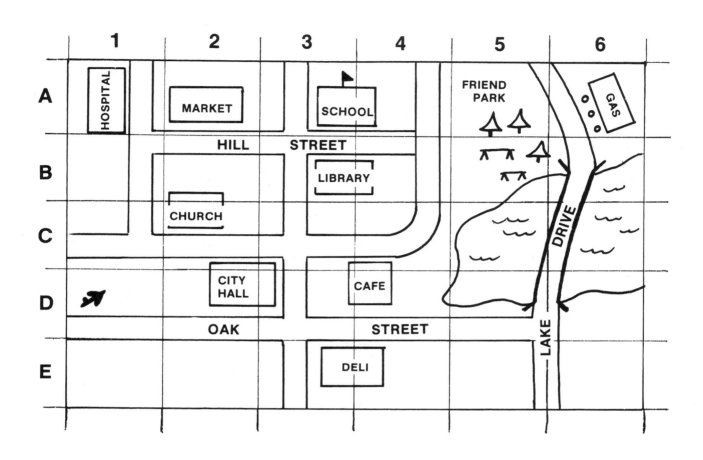

Write the number and letter of the block in which you find the following places. If the place is in more than one block, write all the blocks where it is found.

1. The airport _____
2. The market _____
3. City Hall _____
4. The bridge _____
5. The park _____

6. The library _____
7. The school _____
8. The hospital _____
9. The lake _____
10. The deli _____

What do you find in these blocks?

A6 _____

C2 _____

D4 _____

E1 _____

Now that you know how to use a grid, use it to complete the map below. Be sure to write the name of each place you add to the map.

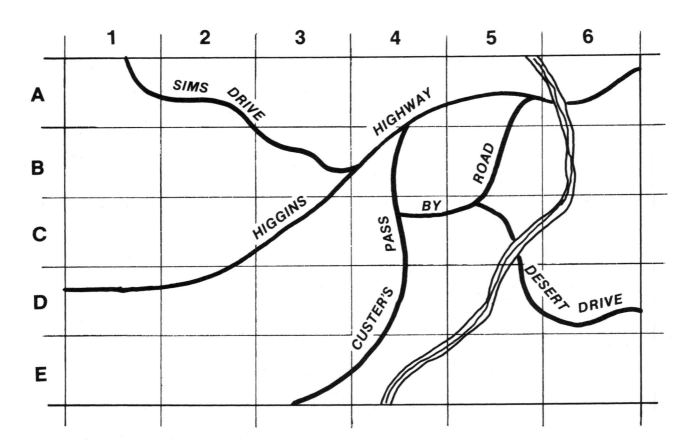

1. There are bridges in **A6** and **C5**.

2. The town of Simsville is in **B2**.

3. Santo National Forest is in **D1 and D2** south of the highway.

4. The city of Oasis is in **D6**.

5. **B1 and C2** are where the Snow Mountains are located.

6. The town of Custer is in **E4**.

7. Holly Lake is in **A4**.

8. The city of Baxton is in **C4**, west of Custer's Pass.

9. **Denton** is a city found in **B5**.

10. The railroad connects the towns of Simsville and Custer.

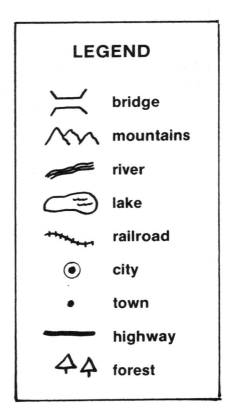

Now let's try using a grid on a map of a real place. Use the map and the grid to answer the questions.

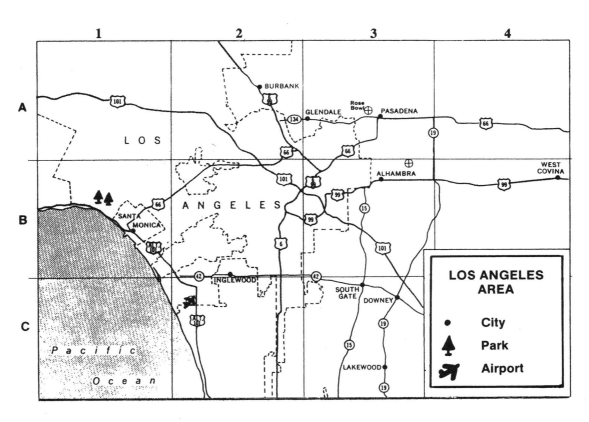

1. What city is in **B4**? _____

2. Where do you find the **Rose Bowl**? _____

3. List the grids in which the **Pacific Ocean** is located. ____ ____ ____

4. Where is the **airport** located? _____

5. Find **U.S. Highway 99**. List the grids it runs through. ____ ____ ____

6. If you were going from **South Gate** to **Inglewood**, in what direction would you go?

_____

7. In what grid is **Glendale**? _____ **Santa Monica**? _____

8. Where do you find the **park**? _____

9. What three cities are in **C3**? _____

_____

10. What direction is **Alhambra** from **Pasadena**? _____

This map shows Glacier National Park in Montana. Use the grid and the map to answer the questions.

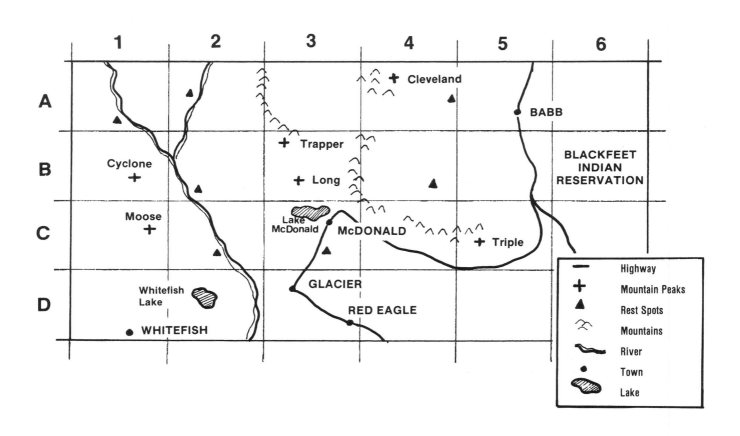

1. In what block do you find Moose Peak? _____

2. Where is Trapper Peak? _____

3. Is there a rest spot in **B2**? _____

4. Find the town of Babb. Where is it? _____

5. Whitefish Lake and the town of Whitefish are not in the same block. Where are they?

   Whitefish Lake _____   Whitefish _____

6. Where is Cyclone Peak? _____

7. In what block do you find the Blackfeet Indian Reservation? _____

8. If you were going from Red Eagle (**D3**) to Lake McDonald, in which direction would you go? _____

9. What peak is in the same block as Trapper Peak? _____

10. Mt. Cleveland is the highest point in the park. Where is it? _____

The band at Ajax Junior High needs new uniforms. They are going to sell candy bars to raise the money. To make sure they call on every house, they want to draw a grid on this map of the neighborhood. You can help them out!

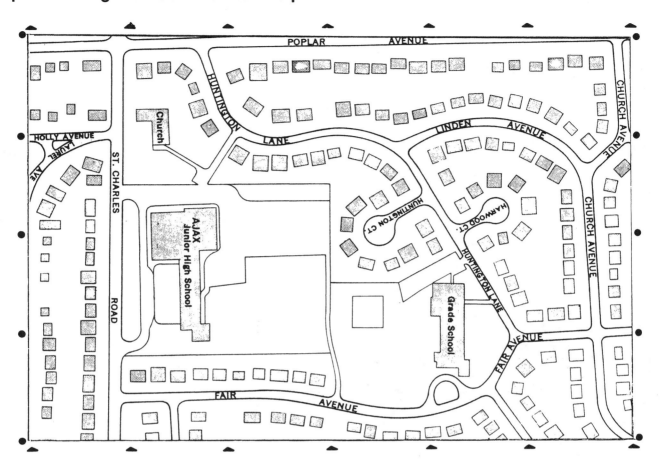

1. Connect the ▲ at the top and bottom of the map.

2. Connect the ● at the sides.

3. Put a number above each space across the top.

4. Put a letter next to each box down the side.

    Answer the questions.

1. Are there any blocks with no houses in them? _____

    Which are they? _____

2. If one band member goes to the houses in **C1** and **D1**, how many houses will he visit?

    _____

3. In which blocks is the junior high? _____   _____   _____

4. How many houses are in **D3**? _____

5. In what block is Harwood Court? _____

6. Where is Laurel Avenue? _____

35

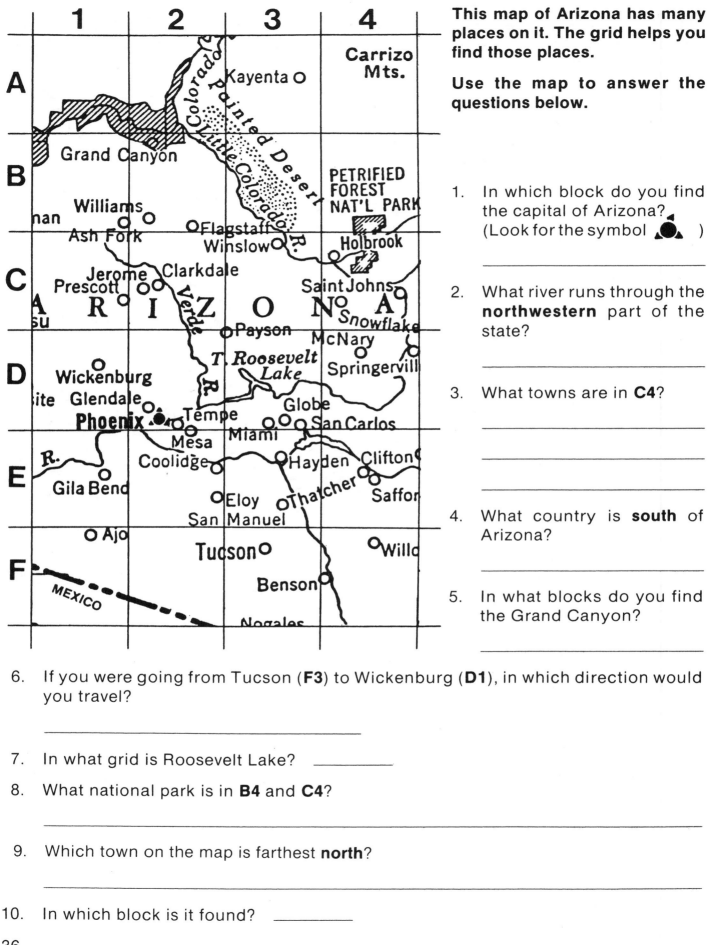

This map of Arizona has many places on it. The grid helps you find those places.

Use the map to answer the questions below.

1. In which block do you find the capital of Arizona? (Look for the symbol ⬤)

_____

2. What river runs through the **northwestern** part of the state?

_____

3. What towns are in **C4**?

_____

_____

_____

4. What country is **south** of Arizona?

_____

5. In what blocks do you find the Grand Canyon?

_____

6. If you were going from Tucson (**F3**) to Wickenburg (**D1**), in which direction would you travel?

_____

7. In what grid is Roosevelt Lake? _____

8. What national park is in **B4** and **C4**?

_____

9. Which town on the map is farthest **north**?

_____

10. In which block is it found? _____

Use the map of Arizona on page 36 to solve these grid mysteries.

Look carefully at each box. Find it on the map. Write the grid location on the line.

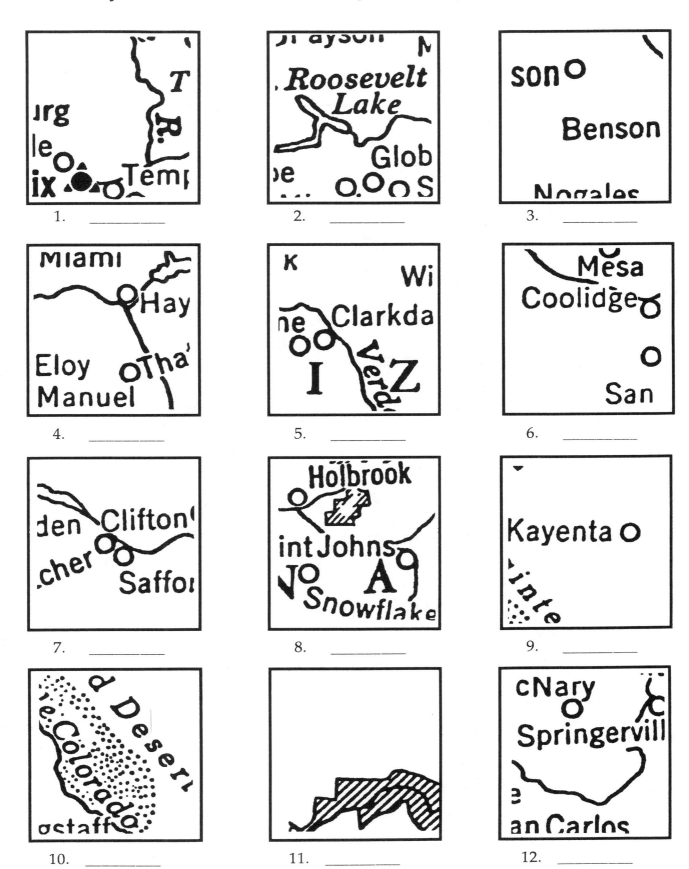

1. _____

2. _____

3. _____

4. _____

5. _____

6. _____

7. _____

8. _____

9. _____

10. _____

11. _____

12. _____

Now, let's look at a map with IMAGINARY grid lines. The letters and numbers are shown, but there are no lines on the map.

You can still find places easily. Just move your finger across to where two lines would meet.

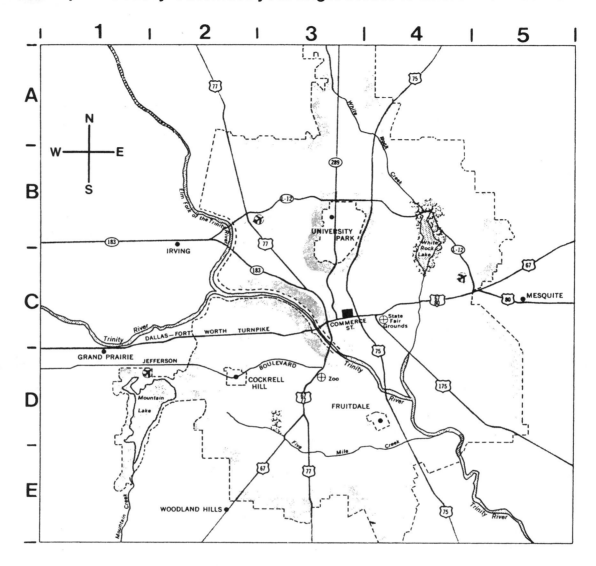

1. In what grids do you find **airports**? _____ _____ _____

2. In what grid is **Woodland Hills**? _____

3. If you were going from the **State Fairgrounds** to **White Rock Lake**, in what direction would you go? _____

4. What **highway** would you take to get from Woodland Hills to Dallas-Fort Worth Turnpike? _____

5. In what grids is **University Park**? _____ and _____

6. What would you find in **D1**? _____

_____

How can you tell how far it is from one place to another by looking at a map? There are two ways. Let's look at one way:

Some maps will have lines drawn from one place to another. Along the lines, numbers will tell you how many miles it is.

Use the map to answer the questions below.

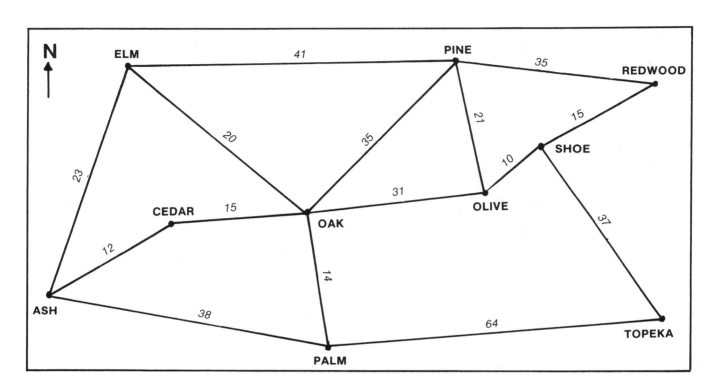

1. How many miles is it from Palm to Oak? _____

2. How many miles is it from Olive to Shoe? _____

3. To go from Olive to Shoe, in what direction would you travel? _____

4. If you went from Elm to Ash and back again, how far would you travel? _____

5. Which trip is shorter — Topeka to Shoe or Pine to Elm?

   _____

6. How much farther is it from Pine to Oak than from Olive to Oak? _____

7. How many miles is it from Ash to Topeka? _____

8. If you travel **northeast** from Ash, what town do you come to first?

   _____

Find the distance from one city to another on this map.

Find **Los Angeles** on the map. Now, find **San Diego**. Look at the number above the line. It is
125. *This tells you that it is 125 miles from Los Angeles to San Diego.*

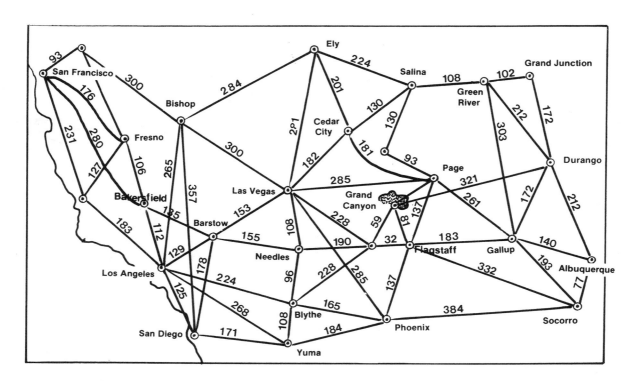

Write the distances for these trips:

1. Barstow to Las Vegas   _____ miles

2. Fresno to San Francisco   _____ miles

3. Needles to Blythe   _____ miles

4. Bishop to Ely   _____ miles

5. Cedar City to Salina   _____ miles

Try these longer trips!

1. Green River to Gallup to Albuquerque.   _____ miles

2. Socorro to Flagstaff to the Grand Canyon.   _____ miles

3. The Grand Canyon to Flagstaff to Las   _____ miles
    Vegas.

4. Grand Junction to Durango to Gallup   _____ miles

5. Los Angeles to San Diego to Yuma   _____ miles

40

Here is part of a United States map. Lines are drawn from place to place. The distance is shown above the line. Use the map to answer the questions below.

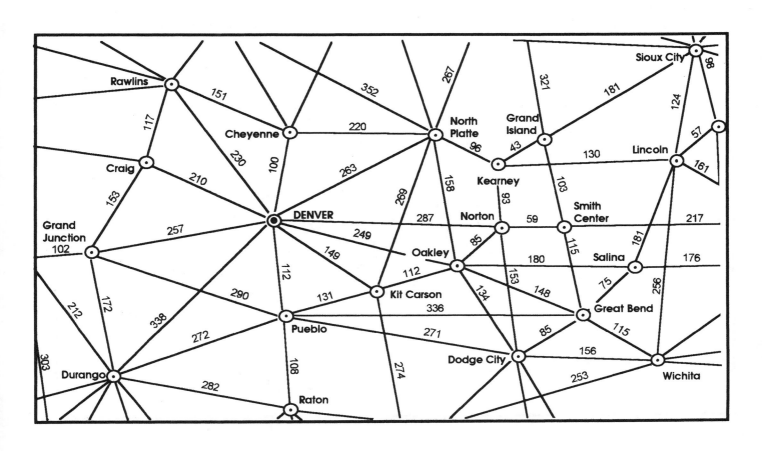

1. How far is it from Kearney to Norton? _____

2. How many miles is it from Kit Carson to Oakley? _____

3. What is the distance from Dodge City to Wichita? _____

4. From Great Bend, it is _____ miles to Smith Center.

5. What direction is Smith Center from Norton? _____

6. Which is closer to Oakley — Denver or Salina? _____

7. If you make a trip from Sioux City to Lincoln and back, how far will you travel?

    _____

8. If you go from Kit Carson to Oakley to Great Bend, how far will you go? _____

9. Which is farther — Cheyenne to Denver or Cheyenne to Rawlins?

    _____

10. How far is it from Durango to Pueblo to Denver? _____

Some maps really make things easy for you. They show the number of miles from one place to another. They also show how much time it will take to drive there!

The map below shows miles AND driving time. The number ABOVE the line is miles. The number BELOW the line tells hours and minutes. (7:25 means 7 hours and 25 minutes.)

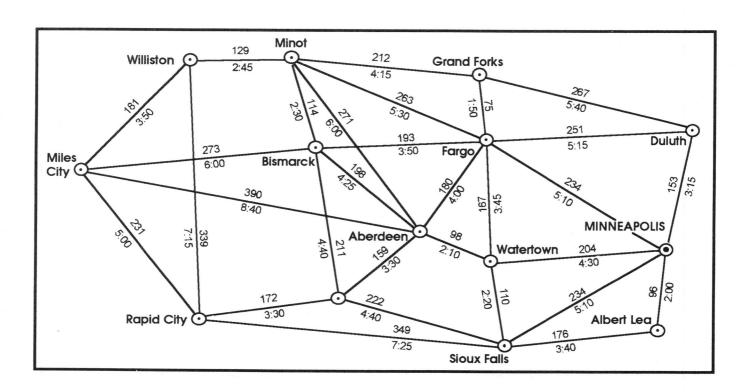

1. How far is it from Rapid City to Pierre? _____ miles

   How long will it take to drive? _____ hours _____ minutes

2. If you went from Aberdeen to Watertown, how long would it take?

   _____ hours _____ minutes

   If you left at 2:00, what time would you get there? _____

3. How long would it take you to get from Miles City to Williston?

   _____ hours _____ minutes

4. If you were going from Sioux Falls to Minneapolis, in what direction would you be

   going? _____

5. Which is closer to Fargo — Duluth or Minneapolis? _____

6. What is the shortest way to get from Pierre to Fargo?

   _____

   How long would the whole trip take? _____ hours _____ minutes

There is another way to measure distance on a map. That way is to use a map SCALE.

It's like a special ruler made just for the map. They come in all different sizes.

This is a map of a small space — an art room. The scale is at the bottom of this page. Cut it out and use it to answer the questions.

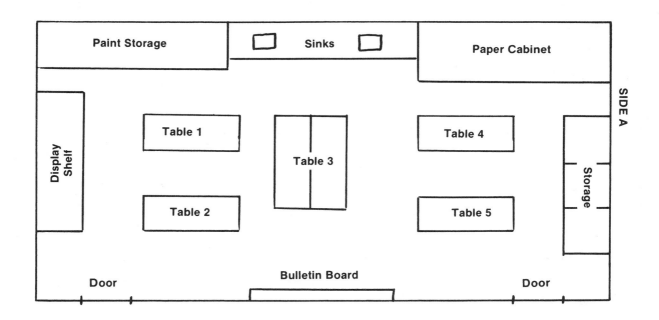

1. How wide is the room along **side A**? _____

2. How far is it from one door to the other? _____

3. How long are the work tables? _____

4. How wide is each of the small storage cabinets? _____

5. How far apart are **Table 1** and **Table 2**? _____

6. How long is the display shelf? _____

Scale:
1 inch = 10 feet

This map scale shows that 1 INCH on the map is the same as 100 YARDS in real space. Use the scale and the map to fill in the blanks. Cut a strip of paper and mark it the same as the scale.

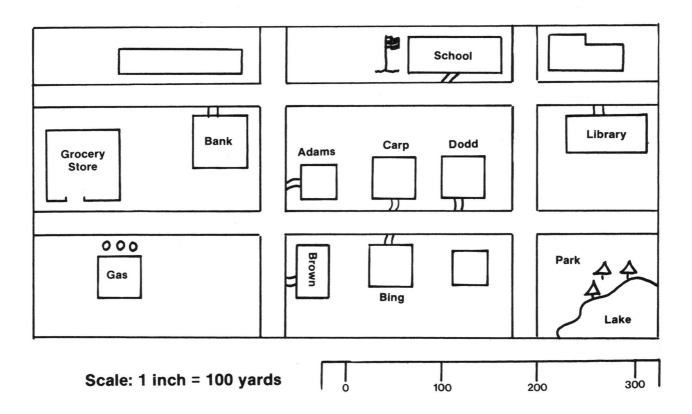

Scale: 1 inch = 100 yards

1. From the Adams' front door to the Brown's is about _____ yards.

2. From the school to the lake is about _____ yards.

3. When Mrs. Dodd goes to the grocery store, she must go about _____ yards.

4. Mr. Adams needed gas for his lawn mower. He walked about _____ yards to the gas station.

5. Jane Carp works at the bank. On her lunch hour, she likes to go to the library.

   How far does she walk? _____ yards

6. Mrs. Bing took her children to the park. They must walk about _____ yards.

7. Mollie Adams must go to the bank to cash a check. It is about _____ yards from her house.

8. Mr. Bing drove his car to the gas station. He drove about _____ yards.

The Smurgle family went on a trip to see their state. They live in the town of Craig. Find Craig on the map. Make an "X" to show where they started their trip.

As you read about their trip and answer the questions, draw a line to show where they went.

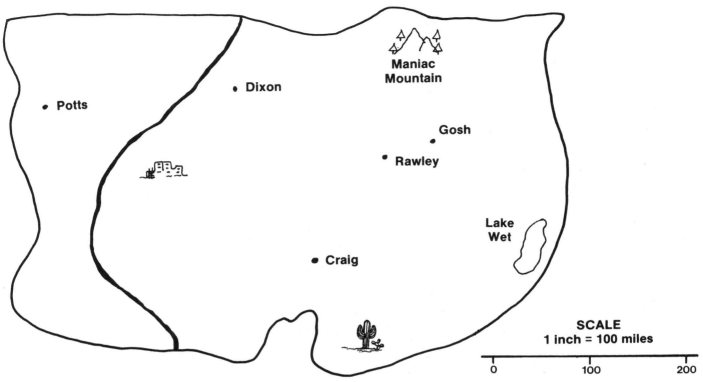

1. They headed **southwest** for 200 miles and camped on the **west** side of State River. Draw a tent where they camped.

2. The next day, they drove to Grandpa Smurgle's house in Potts. How far did they drive?

   _____ miles

3. On the third day, they crossed the river and explored the Indian Ruins.

   They drove _____ miles.

4. Next, they headed for Maniac Mountain and two days of skiing.

   How far was the trip? _____ miles

5. Their next stop was the Rawley Zoo. They drove _____ miles to get there and spent the day.

6. They got as far as Gosh before they had car trouble. How far had they gone?

   _____ miles

7. The car was fixed. They drove as far as the lodge at Lake Wet. How far was that from

   Gosh? _____ miles

8. They drove back through the Sandy Desert and then home. How far did they drive the

   last day? _____ miles

45

Use the map scale to find the answers to the questions below.

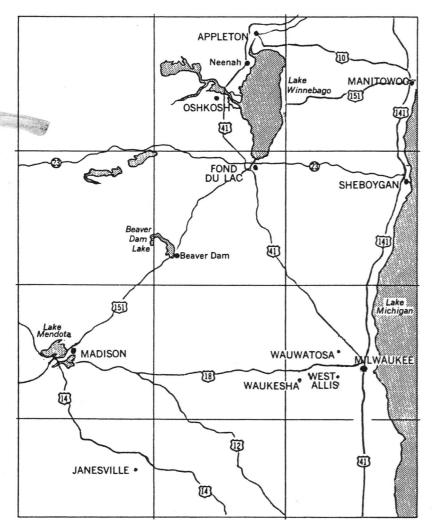

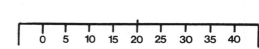

SCALE
1/4 inch = 5 miles / 1 inch = 20 miles

1. About how far is it from Fond du Lac to Milwaukee? _____ miles

2. How long is Lake Winnebago? _____ miles

3. What is the distance from Madison to Beaver Dam? _____ miles

4. How long is Highway 151? _____ miles

5. If you were going from Sheboygan to Oshkosh, in what direction would you travel?

_____

6. What highways would you take? _____   _____

7. How far is it from Janesville to Lake Mendota? _____ miles

8. What highway would you take? _____

This map shows part of the United States. The map scale uses larger numbers because the distances are greater. The scale is 1 INCH = 200 MILES.

Take a strip of paper and mark it the same as the scale. Use the strip to help you measure.

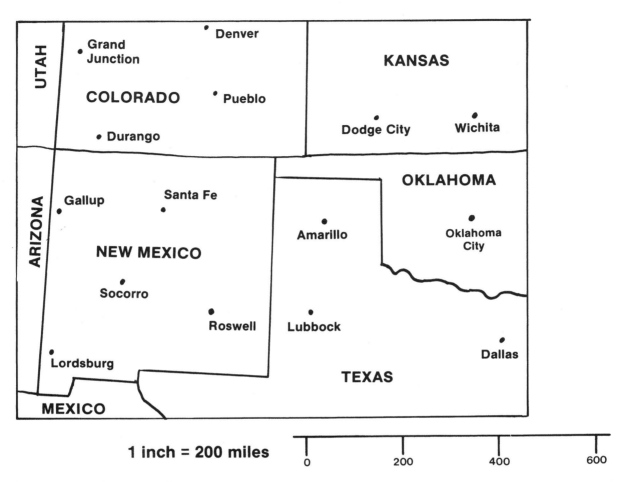

1 inch = 200 miles

What is the distance between:

1. Gallup and Socorro   _____ miles

2. Amarillo and Dallas   _____ miles

3. Denver and Wichita   _____ miles

4. Grand Junction and Durango   _____ miles

5. Dodge City and Oklahoma City   _____ miles

6. Roswell and Lubbock   _____ miles

7. Lordsburg and Gallup   _____ miles

8. Durango and Santa Fe   _____ miles

9. Pueblo and Oklahoma City   _____ miles

Draw a line between each pair of cities. Write the distance ABOVE the connecting line.

We have practiced many map skills — location, symbols, direction, distance. Maps can also tell us lots of other things about a place.

This map of Texas shows the kind of things grown in different parts of the state. The legend will tell you what each area means. Use the map and the legend to answer the questions.

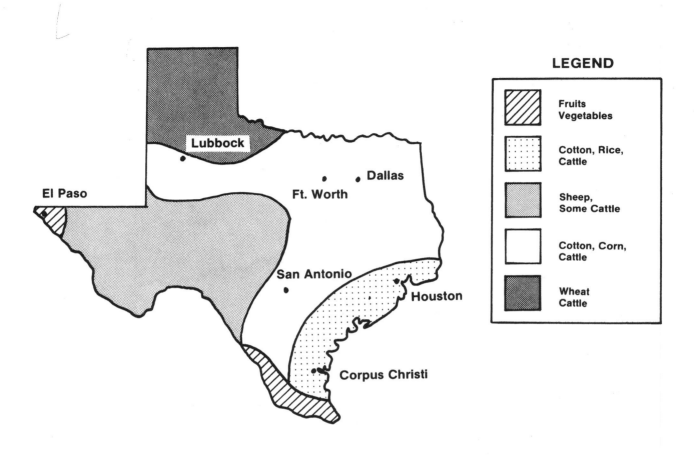

1. What is grown at the **southern** tip of the state?

    _____

2. In what part of the state is wheat grown? _____

3. What big cities are in the area where cotton, corn, and cattle are grown?

    _____

4. What are the main crops near El Paso? _____

5. Near Houston, the main things grown are _____

    _____

6. How many areas raise cattle? _____

7. What is grown on the **eastern** border?

    _____

Picture symbols are also used to give information on maps. This map of the Western United States shows what different places are well-known for. The legend explains each of the picture symbols used. Use the map and the legend to answer the questions.

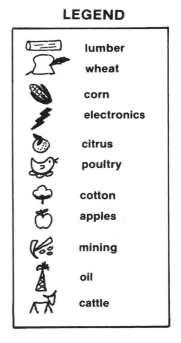

LEGEND

	lumber
	wheat
	corn
	electronics
	citrus
	poultry
	cotton
	apples
	mining
	oil
	cattle

1. What products are found in Oregon?

   _____

2. In what states are electronics important?

   _____   _____

3. What fruit is grown in Washington?   _____

4. In what state is cotton grown?   _____

5. Lumber is important in many states. List the ones shown on the map.

   _____

   _____

6. What is produced in New Mexico?

   _____

7. In what state is mining done?   _____

8. Where is oil found?   _____

This map of California shows how much rain falls each year. The legend tells how to read the map. Use the map and the legend to answer the questions.

1. What part of California (direction) gets the most rain?

   _____

2. About how much rain falls in San Diego each year?

   _____

3. The city on the map that gets the most rain is

   _____

4. Which areas do you think are desert?

   _____

   _____

5. The main thing grown in northern California is trees for lumber. Why would they grow well here?

   _____

   _____

6. How much rain falls in Death Valley each year?

   _____

LEGEND

less than 10 inches

10 - 20 inches

20 - 60 inches

over 60 inches

San Francisco

Sacramento

Monterey

PACIFIC OCEAN

Death Valley

Los Angeles

San Diego

7. Most fruits and vegetables are grown where it rains 10-20 inches a year. What cities are in these areas?

   _____   _____

   _____   _____

8. Wasteland is the name given to places with very little rain. Why is it called "wasteland"?

   _____

   _____

This map shows where people live in the United States. The legend will help you read the map. Use the legend and the map to answer the questions.

Very few

Few

Many

Very Many

1. Do more people live in the eastern or the western half of the United States?

_____

2. Are there more people in Texas or in California?

_____

3. Why do you think there are fewer people living along the southern border of the United States?

_____

_____

4. The area showing very few people that runs from the north to the south is a mountain range. What mountains are these? (Check your atlas.)

_____

5. Find the area where you live. What does the legend tell you about the population?

_____

This is a weather map. It shows what the weather is going to be like on a certain day. The legend will help you understand the map. Use the map and the legend to answer the questions.

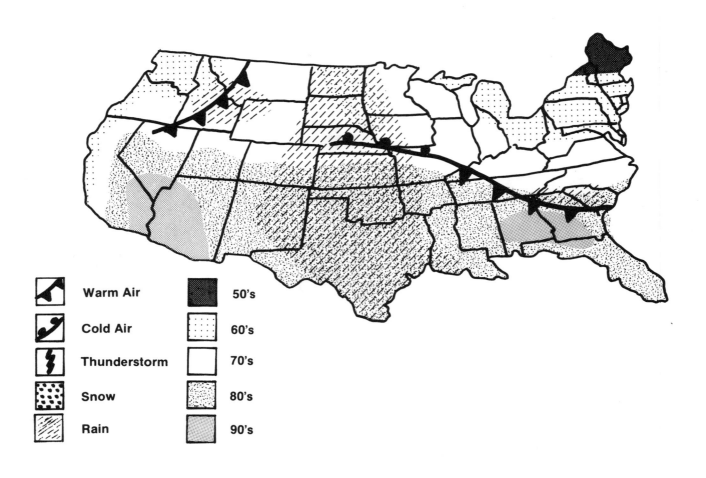

Warm Air

Cold Air

Thunderstorm

Snow

Rain

50's

60's

70's

80's

90's

1. Is it going to rain anywhere? _____ Where? _____

_____

2. Look at the temperatures. What time of year do you think it is? _____

3. If you live in Texas, should you take your umbrella with you today? _____

4. What kind of air is blowing into the South? _____

5. Where is the coldest part of the United States?

_____

6. Is it warmer in Arizona or in Florida? _____

7. What would the weather be like in your state? _____

ANSWER KEY

PAGE 1: First set of four questions: Students should complete compass by placing N,S,E,W in appropriate places. Answer to question 3 is "bottom" and question 4 is "left."
Second set of four questions: 1) left 2) south 3) behind 4) west

PAGE 2: Students should complete both compasses. Teachers make own answer key. 1) north 2) east 3) northeast 4) south 5) west 6) southwest 7) southeast 8) northwest

PAGE 3: 1) northeast 2) southeast 3) monkey/pond 4) northwest 5) snake/pond 6) southwest 7) southwest, west 8) west, snake 9) northeast to pond, then northwest to bear OR head straight north

PAGE 4: 1) southwest 2) east 3) northwest 4) south 5) northeast 1) south 2) northeast 3) Trout Creek 4) Colorado 5) southwest 6) southeast 7) Logan

PAGE 5: 1) north and south 2) southeast 3) Speedy Stop 4) east and west 5) east 6) northwest 7) east 8) west

PAGE 6: Symbols - Column 1: school, lake, railroad, mountains, forest; Column 2: bridge, building, airport, river, highway
1) Reston, Hinkly, Drake, Wabash 2) Skorner 3) east and west 4) north 5) Horton, Clover

PAGE 7: 1) Center Street and Simmons Avenue 2) west 3) east and west 4) southwest 5) south 6) two 7) north 8) northwest

PAGE 8: **Teacher to make own answer key.

PAGE 9: Maps will vary but should include at least six different things and a legend.

PAGE 10: 1) east and west 2) Missouri, Illinois, Indiana 3) Des Moines 4) town 5) 55 6) 64, 65 7) 70 8) Arkansas 9) Mississippi 10) Jefferson City

PAGE 11: 1) four 2) northwest 3) northwest 4) north 5) east, Highway 15 6) Black 7) Warren, Maple Park

PAGE 12: 1) Main Hall 2) east 3) east 4) east or west 5) south on Chuckle Road, east on Tee Hee Trail 6) Arts & Crafts 7) stable 8) west 9) ball field

PAGE 13: 1) Fairview Road 2) east 3) Hog House 4) left 5) bridge 6) south 7) fence 8) southeast 9) southwest 10) west

PAGE 14: 1) Gatesville, Main Street 2) west 3) police department 4) Ajax and Main Street 5) library 6) bank 7) south 8) southeast, Heath Avenue and Ajax 9) northeast 10) variety store

PAGE 15: 1) Big Lake 2) city limits 3) 5, west 4) 67 5) 32 6) three 7) west 8) zoo, falls, museum

PAGE 16: 1) Sandy Way 2) west 3) Beach Avenue 4) Sunny Lake Hotel 5) three 6) market 7) northeast 8) gas 9) Plaza Drive 10) southwestern corner of Sandy Way & Beach Avenue

PAGE 17: 1) seals, elephants, giraffes, zebras 2) seals, monkeys, ducks 3) south 4) Chimp Circle 5) Reptile House 6) fish 7) west 8) reptile house

PAGE 18: 1) Highway 56 2) east 3) Blye to Ray 4) 72 5) Blye, North City, Ray, Gibson 6) south 7) north 8) northeast, Range Road

PAGE 19: **Teacher to make own answer key.

PAGE 20: 1) Independence Avenue and 1st Street 2) east and west 3) Pennsylvania Avenue & 9th Street 4) Constitution Avenue 5) north and south 6) U. S. Capitol 7) Museum of American History and Gallery of Art 8) Pennsylvania Avenue

PAGE 21: 1) Space City 2) Pirate Cove 3) Indian Village 4) Pop's Pizza 5) south and east 6) Wheels-O-Fun 7) northeast, Figby's Farm 8) southeast 9) south 10) west

PAGE 22: 1) Canada; Superior, Michigan, Huron, Erie, Ontario 2) Pacific 3) Montana 4) Texas, Louisiana, Mississippi, Alabama, Florida 5) Alaska, Hawaii

PAGE 23: 1) west to east 2) North Pole 3) South Pole 4) North America, South America, Antarctica, Europe, Asia, Africa, Australia 5) Pacific, Atlantic, Arctic, Indian 6) northern

PAGE 24: 1) Canada, U.S. 2) Canada, U.S., Mexico, Greenland 3) Atlantic 4) Pacific 5) south 6) Canada 7) Arctic 8) south

PAGE 25: 1) South America, Antarctica 2) northern, southern, southern 3) north 4) Atlantic 5) Pacific 6) northern 7) Brazil 8) western

PAGE 26: 1) Europe, Asia 2) Russia 3) west 4) Pacific, Indian, Arctic 5) Arctic 6) Russia 7) Mongolia 8) Japan 9) Africa 10) India

PAGE 27: 1) Africa 2) northern 3) Indian 4) Mediterranean 5) South Africa 6) Atlantic 7) Madagascar 8) Morocco, Algeria, Tunisia, Libya, Egypt

PAGE 28: 1) east 2) Atlantic 3) southwest 4) Pacific 5) Arctic 6) Atlantic 7) South America 8) Africa (Asia or Europe also acceptable) 9) South America, Africa

PAGE 29: **Teacher to make own answer key.

PAGE 30: 1) A2-lake, tree; C5-mountains, road; B3-road, railroad; A3-trees 2) C2, C3, B3, B4, B5, B6, A6 3) D3 4) A5 5) no 6) B6

PAGE 31: 1) D1, C1 2) A2 3) D2, D3, C2, C3 4) D5, D6, C5, C6, B6 5) A5, B5 6) B3, B4 7) A3, A4 8) A1 9) D4, D5, D6, C5, C6, B5, B6 10) E3, E4   A6-street, gas station; C2-church, streets; D4-cafe, lake, street E1-nothing

PAGE 32: **Teacher to make own answer key.

PAGE 33: 1) West Covina 2) A3 3) B1, C1, C2 4) C2 5) B2, B3, B4 6) west 7) A3, B1 8) B1 9) South Gate, Downey, Lakewood 10) south

PAGE 34: 1) C1 2) B3 3) yes 4) A5 5) D2, D1 6) B1 7) B6 8) north or northwest 9) Long 10) A4

PAGE 35: Students should draw grid on map and put appropriate symbols horizontally and vertically. 1) yes - B2, C2, C3 2) 22 3) B2, C2, D2 4) 9 5) B5 6) B1

PAGE 36: 1) D2 2) Colorado 3) Holbrook, Saint Johns, Snowflake 4) Mexico 5) A1, A2, B1, B2 6) northwest 7) D3 8) Petrified Forest 9) Kayenta 10) A3

PAGE 37: 1) D2 2) D3 3) F3 4) E3 5) C2 6) E2 7) E4 8) C4 9) A3 10) B3 11) A1 12) D4

PAGE 38: 1) D1, B2, C4 2) E2 3) northeast 4) 67 5) B3, C3 6) airport, Mountain Lake, Jefferson Blvd., Grand Prairie

PAGE 39: 1) 14 2) 10 3) northeast 4) 46 5) Topeka to Shoe 6) 4 7) 102 8) Cedar

PAGE 40: 1) 153 2) 176 3) 96 4) 284 5) 130   1) 443 2) 413 3) 341 4) 344 5) 296

PAGE 41: 1) 93 2) 112 3) 156 4) 115 5) east 6) Salina 7) 248 8) 260 9) Cheyenne to Rawlins 10) 384

PAGE 42: 1) 172, 3 hours 30 minutes 2) 2 hours 10 minutes, 4:10 3) 3 hours 50 minutes 4) northeast 5) Minneapolis 6) Pierre-Aberdeen-Fargo, 7 hours 30 minutes

PAGE 43: 1) 30 feet 2) 40 feet 3) 10 feet 4) 5 feet 5) 5 feet 6) 15 feet

PAGE 44: 1) 100 2) 300 3) 400 4) 200 5) 400 6) 200 7) 100 8) 250

PAGE 45: 1) Students to draw tent in appropriate spot. 2) 250 3) 150 4) 300 5) 100 6) 50 7) 150 8) 300

PAGE 46: 1) 50 2) 25 3) 30 4) 115 5) northwest 6) 23, 41 7) 35 8) 14

PAGE 47: 1) 200 2) 450 3) 600 4) 200 5) 300 6) 200 7) 300 8) 200 9) 600

PAGE 48: 1) fruits, vegetables 2) northern 3) Dallas, Ft. Worth, San Antonio 4) fruits, vegetables 5) cotton, rice, cattle 6) four 7) cotton, corn, cattle, rice

PAGE 49: 1) poultry, lumber, wheat 2) California, Arizona 3) apples 4) Arizona 5) Washington, Montana, Idaho, Oregon, Nevada, Arizona, New Mexico 6) lumber, wheat 7) Nevada 8) California

PAGE 50: 1) northwest, east central 2) 10-20 inches 3) San Francisco 4) southeast, central 5) lots of rain 6) less than 10 inches 7) Sacramento, Monterey, Los Angeles, San Diego 8) nothing grows well with little rain

PAGE 51: 1) eastern 2) California 3) answers will vary 4) Rocky Mountains 5) answers will vary

PAGE 52: 1) yes, central U.S., southeastern states, northwestern states 2) spring or fall 3) yes 4) warm 5) northeast 6) Arizona 7) answers will vary